Explore!
LONDON

Liz Gogerly

Published in 2015 by Wayland
First published in 2012 by Wayland
Copyright © Wayland 2015

Wayland
338 Euston Road
London NW1 3BH

Wayland Australia
Level 17/207 Kent Street
Sydney, NSW 2000

Editors: Victoria Brooker and Julia Adams
Designer: Elaine Wilkinson
Picture Researcher: Shelley Noronha
Illustrations for step-by-steps: Peter Bull

British Library Cataloguing in Publication Data

London. -- (Explore!)
1. London (England)--Juvenile literature.
I. Series
914.2'1-dc23

ISBN: 978 0 7502 8407 3

Printed in China

Wayland is a division of Hachette Children's
Books, an Hachette UK company

www.hachette.co.uk

Picture acknowledgements:
The author and publisher would like to thank the
following agencies and people for allowing these
pictures to be reproduced:
Cover (top left) Samot/Shutterstock.com (top
right) James Steidl/Shutterstock.com
(bottom left) Birute Vijeikiene/Shutterstock.com
(bottom right) Dave Greenberg/Shutterstock.
com; 4 © Worldwide Picture Library/Alamy; 5
(top) Bikeworldtravel/Shutterstock.com (bottom)
© AA World Travel Library/TopFoto; 6 © Look
and Learn/Bridgeman Art Library; 7 (top) ©
Look and Learn/Bridgeman Art Library (bottom)
Chetham's Library, Manchester, UK/Bridgeman
Art Library; 8 Getty Images; 9 (top) © Nicolaes
Visscher/Getty Images (bottom) World Pictures/
Photoshot; 10 Corporation of London/HIP/
TopFoto; 11 (top) Elena Elisseeva/Shutterstock.
com (bottom) Gustave Dore/Getty Images; 12
© Bettmann/CORBIS; 13 (top) Hulton Archive/
Getty Images (bottom) F Davis/Getty Images;
14 Michael Putland/Getty Images; 15 (top) PA
Photos/TopFoto (bottom) Jonathan Hordle/Rex
Features; 16 Chris Jenner/ Shutterstock.com; 17
(top) Nando Machado/Shutterstock.com (bottom)
cycreation/Shutterstock.com; 20 pcruciatti/
Shutterstock.com; 21(top) Josef78/Shutterstock.
com (bottom) © Jane Sweeney/JAI/Corbis; 22
© Daniel Leal Oliva/Demotix/Corbis; 23 (top)
© John Harper/Corbis, (bottom) Getty BWP
Media/Getty; 24 Rex Features; 25 (top) TopFoto/
Empics (bottom) PA Photos/TopFoto; 26 r.nagy/
Shutterstock.com; 27 (top) godrick/shutterstock.
com (bottom) Padmayogini/Shutterstock.com; 28
Gherkin r.nagy/Shutterstock.com, Underground
tube sign Patrik Mezirka/Shutterstock.com;
London eye Kamira/Shutterstock.com

Contents

London life	4
The birth of London	6
Medieval and Tudor London	8
Enter the Victorian age	10
London under attack	12
Fashionable London	14
City transport	16
Make a London bus	18
Sport in London	20
Learn all about it	22
The people of London	24
The River Thames	26
Facts and figures	28
Glossary	30
Further reading and websites	31
Index	32

London life

London is the capital city of England and the United Kingdom (UK). It is the centre of government for the UK and the home of the royal family. It is also the largest city in Europe, with a population of nearly 8 million people.

Buckingham Palace, in the borough of Westminster, is the residence of the royal family.

London boroughs

London is a city in south-east England. The whole of London is called Greater London and covers about 620 square miles (1.606 square kilometres). It includes Inner London and Outer London. Inner London is made up of twelve boroughs. These include Westminster, where Buckingham Palace and Westminster Abbey are located, and the 'City' of London. This is actually just a small area in the centre of London and is the headquarters for many banks. Outer London is made up of twenty boroughs. Wembley Stadium is in the borough of Brent to the north.

Cosmopolitan city

London is often called the most multi-cultural city in the world. It has the largest non-white population of any European city. There are more than 270 nationalities living in the city and over 300 different languages are spoken. Some parts of London have even been named after the people that have settled there, such as Chinatown in Soho, Little Portugal around Stockwell and Little India in Southall.

Hundreds of visitors flock to Chinatown to celebrate Chinese New Year.

Capital of culture

In 2011, 30.8 million people travelled to London for business and pleasure. Most tourists head to central London to see its famous sights. The London Eye is the most popular paid attraction in the city. London has lots of free museums and galleries including the British Museum, Tate Modern, Natural History Museum, Science Museum and the Victoria and Albert Museum. London is packed with shops, restaurants, theatres and venues, making it one of the top cultural destinations in the world.

The London Eye attracts around 3.5 million visitors every year.

The birth of London

London is an ancient city. Nobody knows exactly when it was first settled but, in 2010, archaeologists discovered some wooden foundations on the shoreline of the river Thames. These have been dated back to about 4,500 BCE.

An artist's impression of how London would have looked in Roman times.

Romans in Britain

The Romans invaded Britain in 43 CE. They built a town beside the river Thames and called it Londinium. They settled here because it was close to the sea and had trading routes to other countries. They built a market square (forum), a large public building (basilica) for the town council, temples, bathhouses, amphitheatres and a wall to protect them against enemy tribes. Archaeologists have discovered some remains in the Square Mile area of the City of London. Parts of the Roman basilica lie in the basement of a hairdresser's shop in Gracechurch Street. Remains of the amphitheatre are hidden under the Guildhall Yard.

Lundenwig

The Romans left Britain in 410 CE. Some historians think that Londinium was probably uninhabited for some years after that. From 450 CE the Saxons, Angles and Jutes moved into the area. These tribes joined together to become the Anglo Saxons and they built their own town called Lundenwig in the Covent Garden area. The Anglo Saxons lived there until the Vikings of Denmark burned Lundenwig to the ground in about 852 CE.

An artist's impression of Anglo Saxons arriving to invade Britain.

The centre of power

The Saxons drove the Vikings out in 886 CE and built a new centre called Lundenburg. The town thrived under Saxon rule but, in 1016 the Saxons were defeated by the Danish leader Canute. In 1042 the Saxon leader Edward the Confessor took the throne back. He built a palace and abbey at Westminster. Today the government meets at the Palace of Westminster (also known as the Houses of Parliament).

Edward the Confessor being crowned in 1042.

Medieval and Tudor London

London continued to grow and prosper within the old Roman walls. Edward the Confessor died in 1066 and was buried at Westminster Abbey. Edward was succeeded by Harold Godwinson – the last of the Anglo Saxon kings.

Norman London

In 1066 the Normans from Normandy in France invaded England. Harold Godwinson was killed at the Battle of Hastings. The Norman leader William II, the Duke of Normandy, took the throne. He was crowned William I at Westminster Abbey on Christmas Day, 1066. The new king, better known as William the Conqueror, built the first Tower of London on the north bank of the Thames. The Tower was a symbol of Norman power and protected the city against rebels. The original structure was replaced with the stone White Tower in about 1078.

The Tower of London as it looked in medieval times.

Medieval London

By the thirteenth century London was a thriving port. The population grew and so did the hustle and bustle of everyday life. Shops and businesses sprang up along London's narrow streets. Rich merchants' houses were built next to the hovels of the poor. In 1257 King Henry III held the first English parliament in Westminster Abbey. By 1300 London had a population of about 70,000. The Black Death reached London in 1348. The disease spread quickly and up to 30,000 Londoners died from it.

London began to expand alongside the Thames. This illustration shows London Bridge.

Tudor times

In Tudor times (1485–1603) London was the largest city in Europe. In 1600 the population had grown to about 250,000. Many of the things that are important to the city today have roots in the Tudor age. Great wooden theatres like the Globe and the Swan were built at Southwark. Many buildings were destroyed during the Great Fire of London in 1666. Fortunately, the fire didn't reach London Bridge or the Tower of London. The George pub in Fleet Street is the only wooden building to have survived the blaze.

The modern reconstruction of the Globe theatre was opened in 1997 near the site of the original Globe theatre.

Enter the Victorian age

The Industrial Revolution which happened partly during the Victorian era (1837–1901) brought forth a time of great change and prosperity. London became the largest city in the world and the international centre for trade and finance.

London grows

The promise of riches and a better life brought people from all backgrounds to London. The population exploded from 1 million to 6.7 million between 1800 and 1900. Much of London's housing was developed in Victorian times. This included grand villas for rich industrialists and rows of terraced houses for the working classes.

Some of the grand houses for rich Victorians in Queen Square, central London.

The Royal Albert Hall, built in Victorian times, is still an important venue for concerts and major events.

London landmarks

Many of London's famous landmarks were built to show off Great British wealth and power. The Houses of Parliament on the banks of the Thames was built in the Gothic style that was popular in Victorian times. The building has more than 1,100 rooms and took thirty years to complete. The Royal Albert Hall in South Kensington was opened in 1871 and named after Queen Victoria's late husband Prince Albert. London also extended outwards. The railway and the underground railway meant faster travel into the city. Villages on the outskirts of London, such as Hampstead and Islington, eventually became part of the city.

Rich and poor Londoners

Britain was the richest nation in the world yet life was hard for London's poorest people. Many poor people lived in overcrowded slums. The Old Nichol in Bethnal Green was the worst slum in Britain. Families lived in one room in rotting tenement blocks. They had no heating and used shared outdoor toilets. Raw sewage poured into cesspits or onto the streets. Death and disease was part of everyday life. Meanwhile, life for the rich was luxurious and comfortable. By the end of the Victorian era many rich Londoners had hot running water and flushing toilets in their homes.

Bare-footed children played in the streets between overcrowded slums.

London under attack

At the start of the twentieth century the British Empire was the most powerful in the world. London was the centre of the empire and people from all over came to the city to live. By 1911 its population had grown to 7.2 million people.

The modern city

By now London had transformed into a modern city. Many streets had electric lighting and there was an efficient sewage system. Motorized buses had taken over from horse-drawn carriages. Slums like the Old Nichol in the east end of London had been demolished and replaced by new council estates. The luxurious Ritz hotel opened in 1906. In 1908 London hosted its first Olympic Games at White City Stadium in West London.

The finish line of the 200 metre race at the London 1908 Olympics.

A zeppelin leaving its German base for a raid on London.

The Great War

The main threat to the British Empire came from Germany. On 4 August 1914 the First World War (the Great War) broke out and London was under attack. In May 1915 the Germans began dropping bombs on the city using Zeppelin airships. By the end of the war in 1918, 650 Londoners had died in German air raids. London also lost thousands of troops overseas. The day the war ended Big Ben in Westminster rang out for the first time since 1914. The Cenotaph in Whitehall was built in 1919 to commemorate British servicemen that died fighting in the war.

The Blitz

In September 1939 the Second World War broke out. Immediately, millions of people were evacuated from London to protect them from air raids. Over 1 million children left the city by train. On 7 September 1940 German planes bombed the Port of London in the East End. German bombers attacked the city every night until 10 May 1941. Blitzkrieg is a German word meaning 'lightning war'. Londoners called these attacks the Blitz. In 1944 and 1945 Germany attacked London with V-1 flying bombs and V2 rockets. By the end of the war 32,000 Londoners had lost their lives and over a million homes had been destroyed.

Soldiers clearing the debris outside Bank Underground Station, after it had been bombed in the Second World War.

Fashionable London

Throughout its history London has attracted rich, creative and fashionable people. In the twentieth century London became famous for its arts, music and fashion scenes.

The 'Swinging Sixties'

In the 1960s young, fashionable people from all over the world came to what would become known as 'Swinging London'. Young women were wearing daring short skirts called 'the mini' designed by Mary Quant. Style icons like the London-born model Twiggy made the mini-skirt even more popular. Meanwhile, British bands like the Rolling Stones and the Beatles were top of the pops all over the world but lived in London.

Mini-skirts were seen as very daring in the 1960s.

Vivienne Westwood's (centre) designs are world-renowned.

Fashion scene

London in the twenty-first century is still a fashionable place to be. London Fashion Week is considered to be one of the 'Big Four' fashion weeks in the world. London designers like Vivienne Westwood, Stella McCartney and the late Alexander McQueen are internationally famous. Meanwhile, London street style often sets the trends.

Art in London

London has some of the most famous art colleges in the world. There have also been some famous art movements based in the city. The London School from the 1970s was founded by artists such as Lucien Freud, Francis Bacon and David Hockney. In the late 1980s a group of artists began exhibiting their works together. Damien Hirst and Tracey Emin became the most successful artists in the movement that is known as Britart. More recently London has become famous for its street art. Camden, Hackney, Tower Hamlets and Leake Street in Waterloo are popular places to discover the work of street artists like Banksy, Ben Eine and Shepard Fairey.

A new work of art by Banksy appeared overnight on this Islington pharmacy.

City transport

From London red buses to black cabs and the London Underground, there are plenty of ways to get to where you want to be in London. Major international airports mean London is also a gateway to the world.

London buses

The London red bus is an icon of the city. Motor buses arrived in 1904 and the first double-decker buses hit the streets in 1925. The most famous kind of London bus is the Routemaster double-decker that appeared in 1959. It had an open doorway at the back so passengers could jump on and off the bus. Most Routemaster buses were taken out of service in 2005. Londoners missed these old buses so much that in 2012 the Routemaster II was introduced.

This new bus has three doors, including an open platform at the back.

Taxi!

London black cabs are famous around the world for their unique style and design. Motor taxis arrived in 1903 and the black cabs were introduced in 1958. Taxi drivers have to pass a special test called 'the Knowledge' that shows that they know 320 routes around the city. London roads are very busy and from 2003 people who want to drive into the centre of the city of London have to pay a fee. London is the first major city in the world to introduce a congestion fee and the money raised is used to extend the public transport system. Licensed taxi drivers do not have to pay the charge.

If the front 'Taxi' light is on, it means the taxi is available for hire.

The first Underground

The London Underground is the oldest underground railway in the world. The first stretch of line (Metropolitan Line), running between Paddington and Farringdon, opened in January 1863. By the 1930s the underground system extended throughout the city. Londoners called the railway system 'the Tube' because most trains travelled through tunnels. The famous Tube map was designed by Harry Beck in 1933. He based the map on an electrical circuit and gave each line its own colour. The map is still used today and has been copied by many underground networks around the world. Today, there are 11 tube lines in the Greater London area served by 270 stations.

The London Underground carries more than 1,107 million passengers every year.

17

Make a London bus

Make your own model of the famous London red bus. You will need an empty washing-powder box. If you can't find one, just use a similar-sized box. If you can't find cotton reels for the wheels, then try bottle tops or empty tealight candle holders.

You will need:

1 empty box measuring no wider than the length of your pencils

4 empty cotton reels

2 pencils measuring about 1 cm longer than the width of the bus

Red paint

Black marker pen

Modelling clay (plasticine)

Paint brushes

Sticky tape

Scissors

1 Draw around the top half of a cotton reel on to the bottom of the box to create the shape of a wheel arch. Cut out four wheel arches.

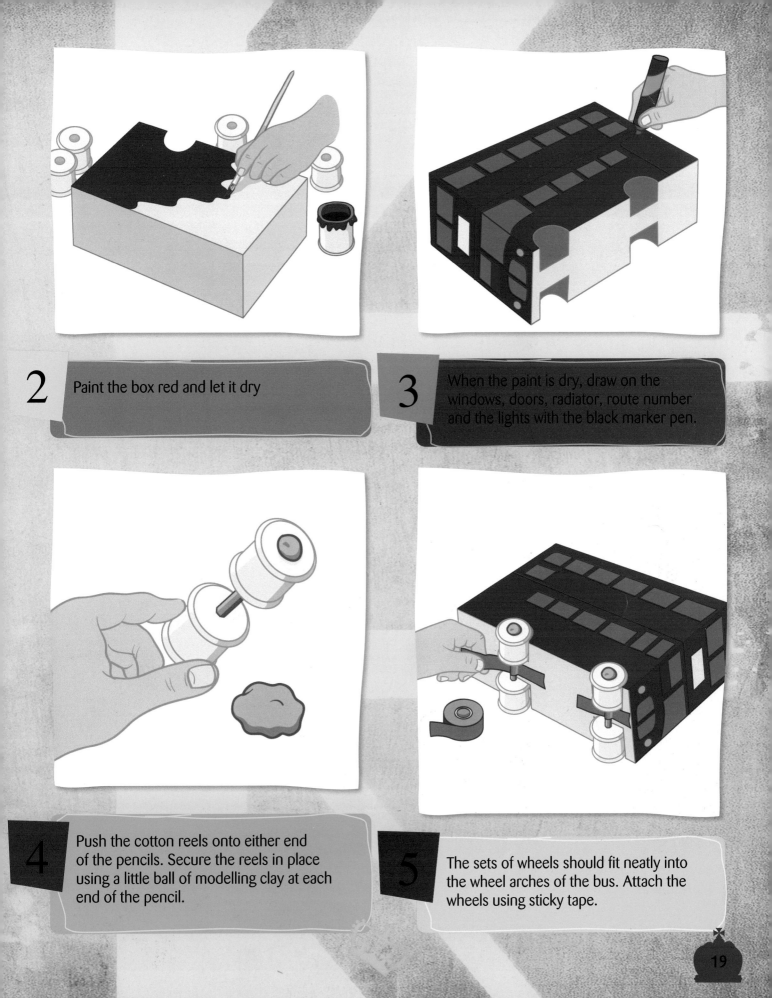

2 Paint the box red and let it dry

3 When the paint is dry, draw on the windows, doors, radiator, route number and the lights with the black marker pen.

4 Push the cotton reels onto either end of the pencils. Secure the reels in place using a little ball of modelling clay at each end of the pencil.

5 The sets of wheels should fit neatly into the wheel arches of the bus. Attach the wheels using sticky tape.

Sport in London

The big city has a long history of hosting top sporting events. The London Marathon and the Oxford and Cambridge Boat Race are just a few of the events that draw the crowds.

The Velopark is one of the lasting legacies of London 2012.

Olympic fever

In 1908 London hosted its first Summer Olympics Games. The Summer Olympics returned to the capital in 1948. It was the first games to be held after the Second World War. They were called the Austerity Games because there was no money for new venues or an Olympic Village for the athletes. Many Londoners rose to the occasion and volunteered to help for free or offered free lodging to the athletes. In 2012 London hosted the Summer Olympics and the Paralympic Games again. Many new venues were built on waste ground or old industrial areas. These sport complexes will be used by Londoners for many years to come.

Anyone for tennis?

Every summer the All England Lawn Tennis and Croquet Club in Wimbledon holds the Championships (also known as Wimbledon). This tournament has been held at the club since 1877 and it is the oldest tennis tournament in the world. The Championships take place over two weeks at the end of June and first week of July every year.

Centre Court at Wimbledon has a retractable roof in case it rains.

Wembley Stadium is the second-largest stadium in Europe.

'On our way to Wembley'

In 1863 twelve football clubs met at the Freemason's Tavern in Great Queen Street, London, to agree rules for the game. Shortly afterwards, the Football Association was founded and an official set of rules were drawn up. The oldest football club in London is Fulham, which started in 1879. These days there are fourteen professional teams in London including Arsenal, Chelsea and Tottenham. Matches between London clubs are called a London Derby and are extremely competitive. London's new Wembley Stadium is the largest covered football stadium in the world. It is the venue for many national and international games.

Learn all about it

London has some of the best-known universities and some of the oldest and biggest libraries in the world. Its museums are packed full of amazing artefacts from different eras, civilisations and cultures.

Colombia's president, Juan Manuel Santos, answering students' questions at the London School of Economics in 2011.

Seats of learning

London is an international centre for education. There are 46 universities, colleges and schools offering higher education. The University of London and Imperial College London are ranked amongst the top universities in the world. The London School of Economics and Political Science (LSE) is another respected college. Many international heads of states and prime ministers have studied there including John F Kennedy, President of the United States (1961–1963) and Juan Manuel Santos, President of Colombia (2010–present). The Royal Academy of Dramatic Art (RADA) is a famous drama school. Its past students include Clive Owen, Maggie Gyllenhaal and Michael Sheen.

London libraries

London has some of the biggest libraries in the world. The London Library in St James's Square was founded in 1841 and is the world's largest independent library. Membership is open to everyone. Borrowers can choose from over one million books and periodicals in 50 different languages. The British Library on the Euston Road has over 150 million books including the first copies of works by Shakespeare and the diaries of Captain Scott. It also houses the Magna Cartna and lyrics by the Beatles.

The British Library receives a copy of every book published in the UK and Ireland.

You can get up close to the moving model of a T-Rex at the Natural History Museum.

Amazing museums

The most popular museum in London is the British Museum. On average more than 5 million people pass through its doors every year. Visitors can see galleries devoted to different cultures of the world. The Natural History Museum on Exhibition Road, Kensington, is another favourite. It's famous for its collection of dinosaur skeletons and the model of a blue whale that measures 25 metres long! A trip to the Science Museum, also on Exhibition Road, is a great way to learn about the Industrial Revolution. Visitors can see Puffing Billy, the oldest surviving steam locomotive and Stephenson's Rocket, the earliest successful locomotive.

The people of London

In the past people said that a true Londoner needed to be born within hearing distance of the bells of St Mary-le-Bow in Cheapside, East London. These days a Londoner refers to anybody from the Greater London area.

What's a Cockney?

A Cockney is an old term for a working-class person from the East End of London. In Victorian times some East-End street sellers spoke in a secret code replacing some words they used with words or phrases that rhymed with the word instead. This way of speaking became known as Cockney Rhyming Slang.

Adam and Eve = believe
"I don't Adam and Eve it!"

Apples and pears = stairs
"Up the apples"

Brown bread = dead
"He was brown bread"

For over 100 years, each London Borough has a Pearly King and Queen. They wear clothes decorated with pearl buttons and raise money for London-based charities.

Multi-cultural Londoners

London has always attracted immigrants from overseas. After the Second World War black and Asian people were encouraged by the British government to seek employment in Britain. Thousands of Jamaicans settled in south London in places like Brixton. A large community of Nigerians settled around Peckham. War in Bangladesh brought a wave of Bengali immigrants in the 1970s. Many of these people settled in the East End, especially Brick Lane. From the late twentieth century a new dialect could be heard on the streets of London. It is called Multicultural London English (MLE) and is made up from Caribbean, Asian and African languages.

A traditional Hindu dancer performs on stage in London at a Diwali festival.

The royal family

Buckingham Palace in Westminster has been the official London residence of the royal family since 1837 when Queen Victoria took the throne. Today, it is the home of the Queen and Prince Philip, Prince Andrew, Prince Edward and his wife Sophie, the Countess of Wessex. Kensington Palace is another important royal residence. It was the home of Princess Diana and Princess Margaret. It is set to become the London home of Prince William and Catherine (Kate), Duchess of Cambridge.

The wedding of Prince William and Kate Middleton attracted huge crowds to London.

The River Thames

London has grown up and developed along the River Thames. Some of the city's most famous landmarks are built along its banks. The Port of London on the Thames was once the largest port in the world.

A mixture of cargo boats and tourist boats crowd the busy Thames waterways.

Trade and industry

The Romans were the first people to build a port in London. The original wharfs were built downstream of London Bridge. The port expanded over the centuries along Billingsgate on the south side of the City of London. In the eighteenth century, the Port of London stretched for miles along both banks of the river. During the Industrial Revolution exports of British goods boomed and the Thames became congested with river traffic. In Georgian and Victorian times the Docklands were developed further east in places like the Isle of Dogs and Wapping. By the twentieth century London's Docklands was a centre for manufacturing and shipbuilding.

Pollution and wildlife

In Victorian times the Thames was badly polluted with human and industrial waste. During the hot summer of 1858 the state of the river was so bad it created a foul smell. If anyone fell into the river they often died from poisoning. This unpleasant time in London's history is known as the 'Great Stink'. Thanks to better sewer systems and efforts to clean up the river the Thames is now the cleanest river in any city in Europe. More than 100 different kinds of fish have been recorded in the river including bream, perch, eel, bass and trout.

Grey herons can be found along many parts of the Thames.

The river today

In the twenty-first century the Thames has seen many changes. In 1982 the Thames Barrier was erected to protect central London from flooding. The former Docklands have also been redeveloped and turned into new homes and offices. Canary Wharf on the Isle of Dogs has become a major business district and has some of the highest skyscrapers in the UK – One Canada Square is the second tallest building in the country.

The UK's first urban cable car service running across the Thames opened in June, 2012

Facts and figures

The Shard is the tallest building in the European Union at 310 metres (1,106 feet) high.

The Theatre Royal in Drury Lane is the oldest theatre still in use in the city and dates from 1812.

The Gherkin in the Square Mile got its name because of its shape. It was designed by Norman Foster and measures 180 metres (590 feet) tall.

The bearskins worn by the Queen's Foot Guards are made of real bearskin, weigh 1.51lbs and are 45.7 cm (18 inches) tall.

The North Greenwich Arena is the largest dome of its kind in the world.

Hot in the city!

In the past London had a reputation for being foggy or rainy. In fact, according to the Met Office, London is the fifth sunniest place in the UK. London has its own microclimate. It gets warmer in the city because of the build up of heat energy emitted from buildings. At the same time this can cause more cloud cover, rain and thunder!

Baker Street Underground Station was built in 1863 and is the oldest underground station in the world!

Campden Hill Square, in Holland Park, is the most expensive street to live in London. In 2012, a house on this road cost on average £4.86 million.

There are 24 bridges that cross the River Thames between Kew Bridge and Tower Bridge. Millennium Bridge, the footbridge between City and Bankside, was opened in 2000 and is the newest bridge in the city.

Glossary

air raids A series of attacks by aircraft dropping bombs and rockets.

amphitheatre An oval or round building with a central arena for the performers surrounded by tiers of seats for the spectators.

austerity Describes a state of having reduced money and less goods.

Black Death The outbreak of bubonic plague that spread through Europe and Asia in the fourteenth century.

British Empire The countries and territories that were formerly under British control.

cesspit A large hole used for storing sewage.

commemorate To remember someone or something.

council estate An area of public or social housing provided by the local council for unemployed or low-paid working people.

foundations The base of a building, usually below ground level.

Great Fire of London The fire that destroyed central parts of London between 2–5 September 1666.

icon A person or object that stands out and becomes a symbol of a certain period of history or a place.

Industrial Revolution The development of factories, machinery and industry that started in the late eighteenth century in England.

industrialist Someone who owns or manages an industrial business.

landmarks Geographical features, monuments, buildings or other structures that stand out in an area.

renowned Famous, known and praised by many people.

residence A house or any other place where people live.

sewage Waste water, human urine or solid waste.

skyscraper A very tall building.

street art Art carried out in public places, especially graffiti, street installations, sculpture and poster art.

tenement A large building in an urban area where poor families could rent rooms.

terraced A row of houses joined to one another.

urban Describes part of a city or town.

velopark A cycling centre with a track for racing.

Further reading

BOOKS

Fiction

A Walk in London by Salvatore Rubbino (Walker, 2012)

Jammy Dodgers on the Run by Bowering Sivers (Macmillan Children's Books, 2005)

The Ruby in the Smoke by Philip Pullman (Scholastic, 2006)

The Secret of Platform 13 by Eva Ibbotson (Macmillan Children's Books, 2009)

Non Fiction

Children's History of London by Jim Pipe (Hometown World, 2011)

50 Things to Spot in London (Usborne Spotter's Cards) by Rob Lloyd Jones (Usborne, 2010)

London (See Inside) by Rob Lloyd Jones (Usborne, 2007)

London Unlocked by Emily Kerr, Joshua Perry and Katherine Hardy (Factfinder Guides, 2010)

Not For Parents: London: Everything you ever wanted to know (Lonely Planet Publications, 2011)

The Story of London by Richard Brassey (Orion's Children, 2009)

Websites

The official London city guide
http://www.visitlondon.com/

Tourist information UK
www.tourist-information-uk.com/

Information about getting around the city
Transport for London:
http://www.tfl.gov.uk/

Regular updates and reports about new discoveries and reports about London's past
from the Museum of London:
http://www.museumoflondonarchaeology.org.uk/NewsProjects/

Suggestions of activities and places to go in the city from London's listing guide:
http://www.timeout.com/london/kids/

Index

air raid 13, 30
Anglo Saxons 7, 8
art 14, 15, 30

Bacon, Francis 15
Banksy 15
Beatles (the) 14, 23
black cabs 17, 16, 17
Black Death 9, 30
Blitz (the) 13
Brick Lane 25
Britart 15
British Empire 12, 13, 30
British Library 23
British Museum 5, 23
Buckingham Palace 4, 25

Canary Wharf 27
Chinatown 5
'City' of London 4
cockney 24
congestion fee 17

Diana, Princess of Wales 25
Docklands 26, 27
Duchess of Cambridge 25

East End 12, 13, 24, 25
Edward the Confessor 7, 8
Emin, Tracey 15

Fairey, Shepard 15
fashion 14–15
First World War 13
Freud, Lucien 15

Globe (the) 9
Godwinson, Harold 8
government 4, 7, 25
Great Fire of London 9, 30

Great Stink (the) 27
Greater London 4, 24

Henry III, King 9
Hirst, Damien 15
Hockney, David 15
Houses of Parliament (Palace of
  Westminster) 7, 11

Industrial Revolution 6, 23, 26,
  30
Isle of Dogs 26, 27

Kensington Palace 25
Knowledge (the) 17

Londinium 6, 7
London Bridge 9, 26
London bus 12, 16, 18–19
London Eye 5 29
London Marathon 20
London Underground 11, 13, 16,
  17, 29
Lundenberg 7
Lundenwig 7

medieval times 8–9
McCartney, Stella 15
McQueen, Alexander 15
Millennium Bridge 29
multi-cultural 5, 25
museum 5, 22, 23

Natural History Museum 5, 23
Normans 8

Olympic Games 20
Oxford and Cambridge boat race
  20

Paralympic Games 20
Pearly King and Queen 24

pollution 27
port 9, 13, 26

Quant, Mary 14

railways 11
River Thames 26–27
Rolling Stones 14
Romans 6, 7, 8, 26
Royal Albert Hall 11
royal family 4, 25

Saxons 7
Science Museum 5, 23
Second World War 13, 20, 25
Shakespeare, William 23
slum 11, 12
sport 20–21

Tate Modern 5
Tower of London 4, 9
transport 16–17
Tube map 17
Tudor times 8–9

universities 22

velopark 20
Victoria and Albert museum (V&A)
  5
Victorian age 10–11, 24, 26, 27
Vikings 7

Wembley Stadium 4, 21,
Westminster 4, 7, 9, 13, 25
Westminster Abbey 4, 8
Westwood, Vivienne 15
wildlife 27
Wimbledon 21
William the Conqueror 8